Blank Comics Book

This comic book
belongs to

KIDS PLAY COMICS

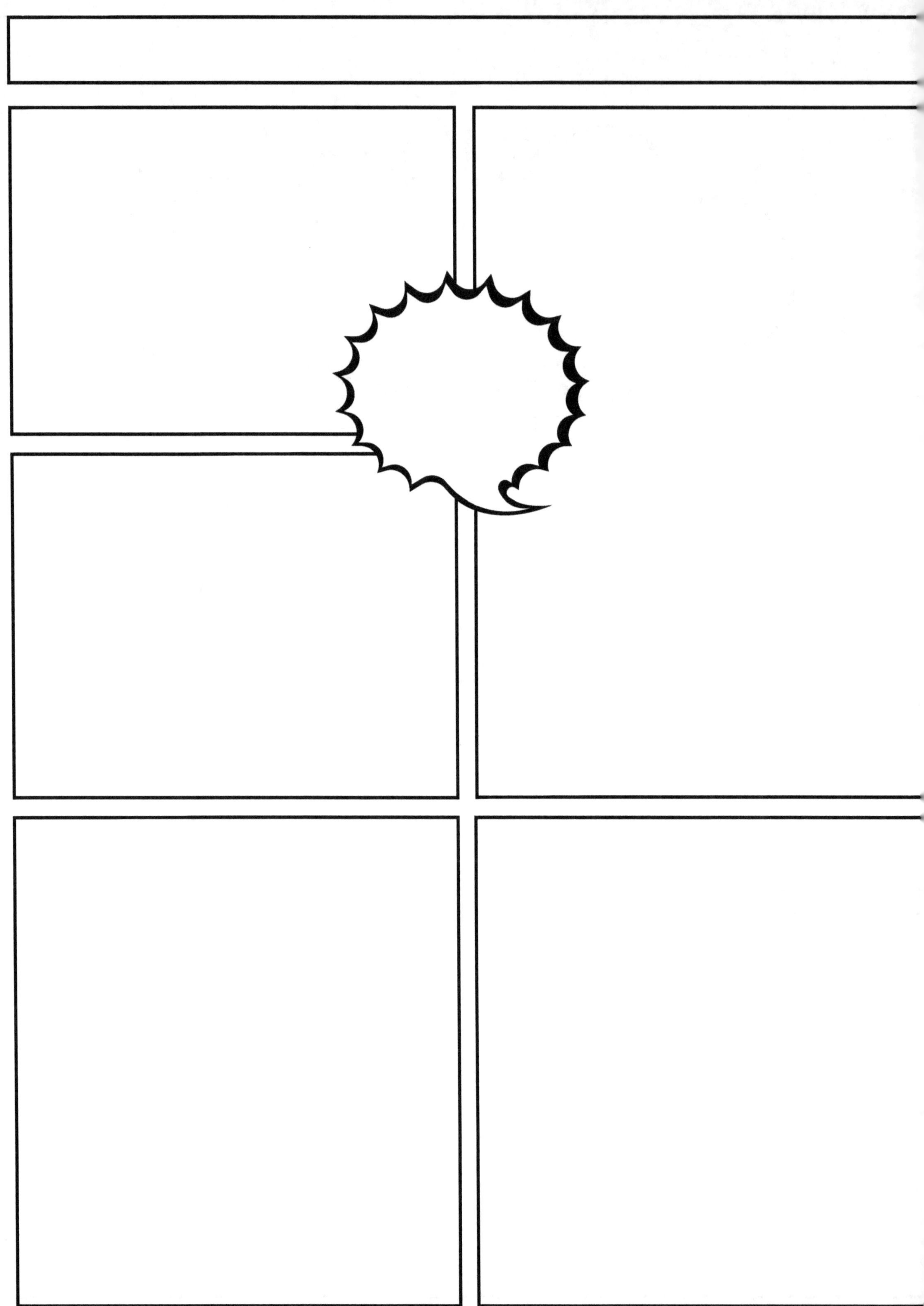

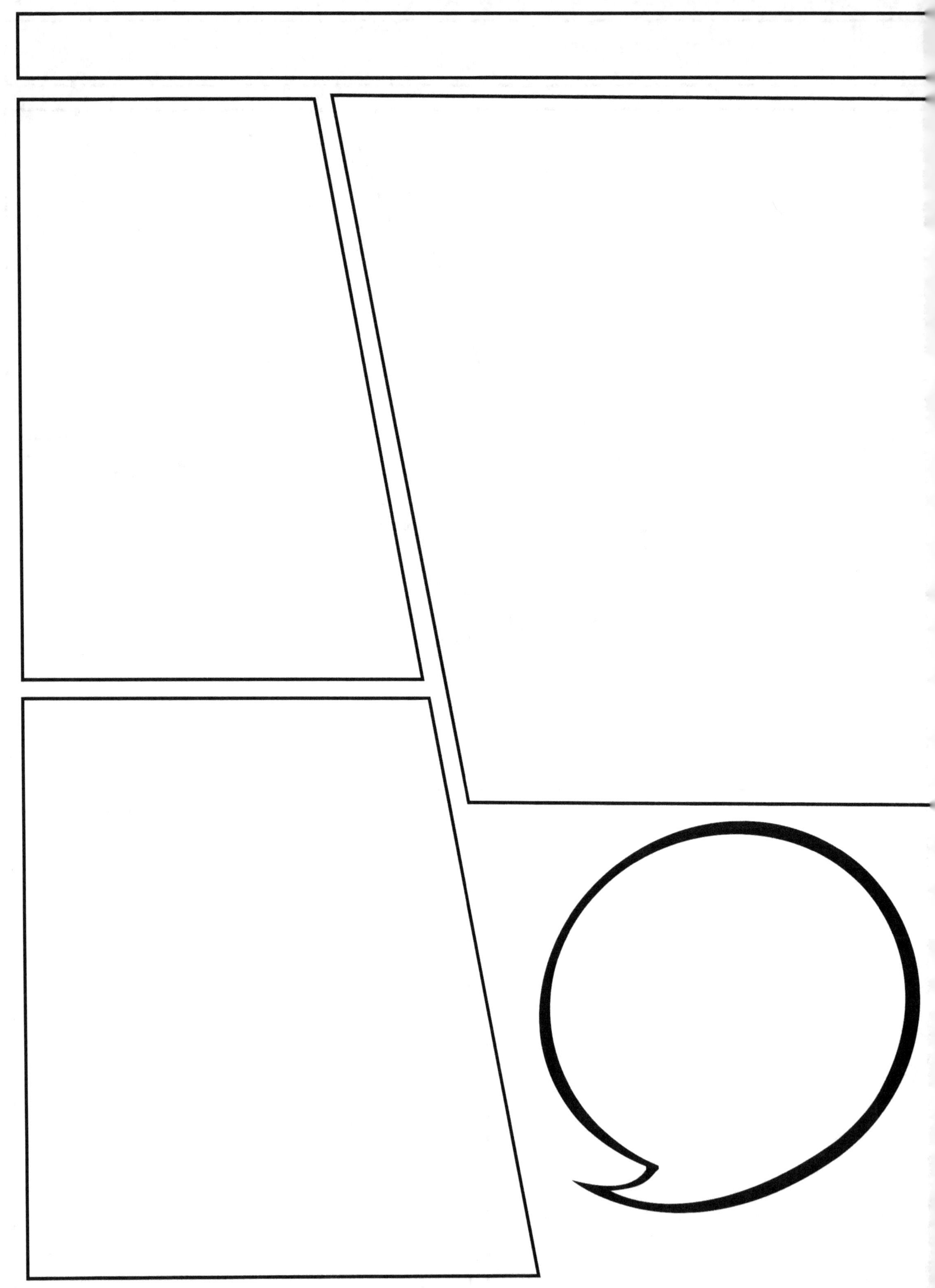

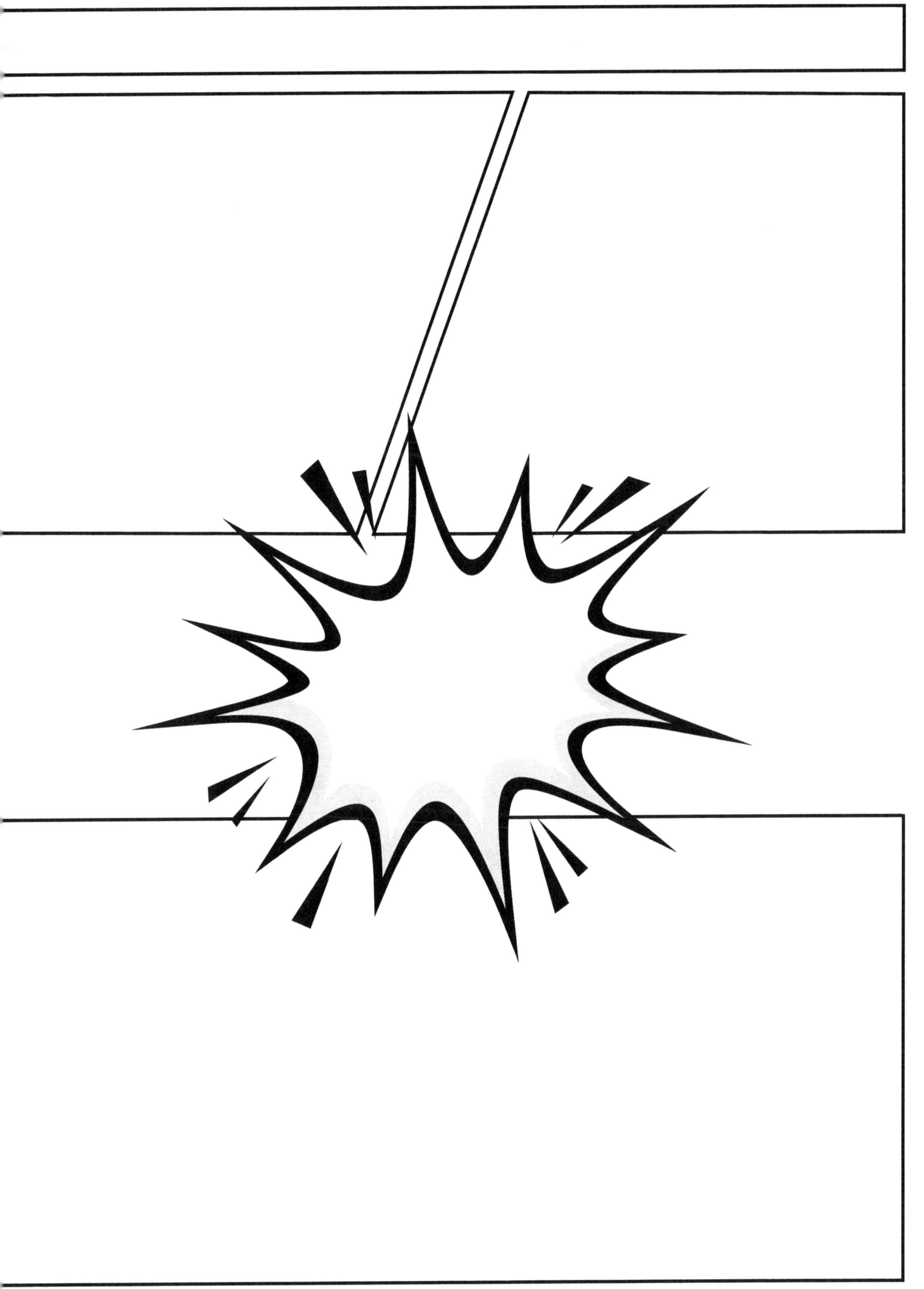

?
BOOM

WOW!

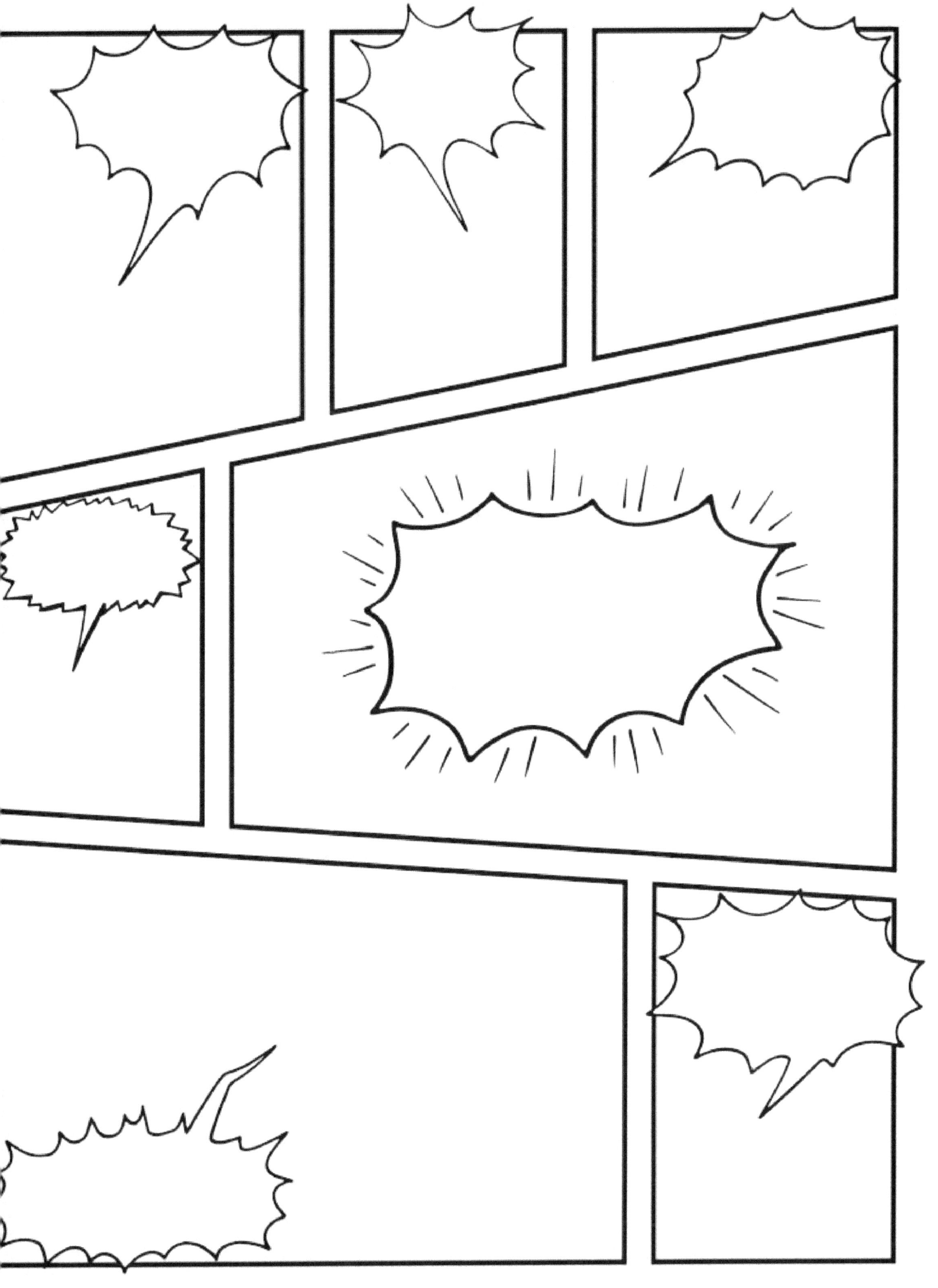

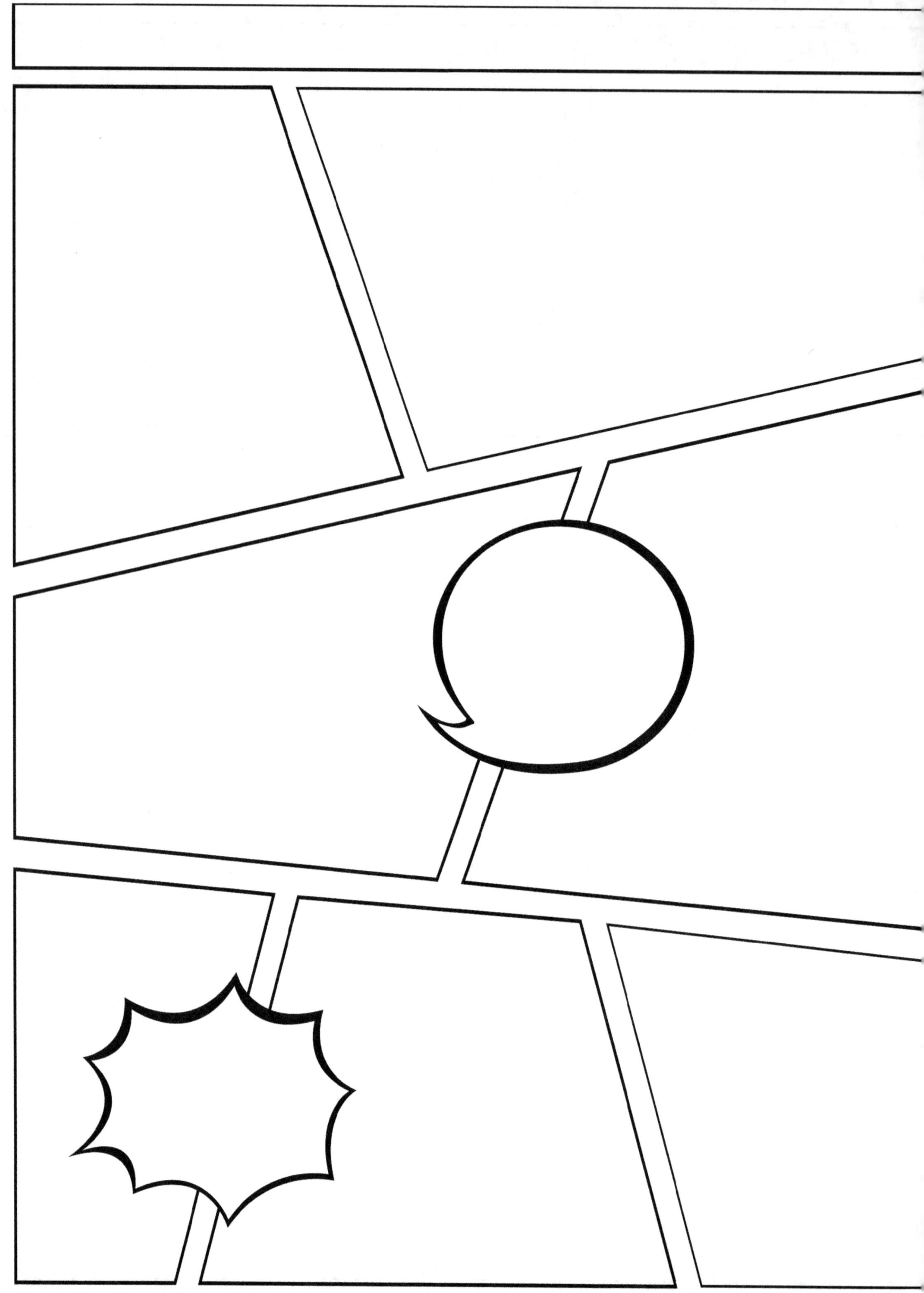

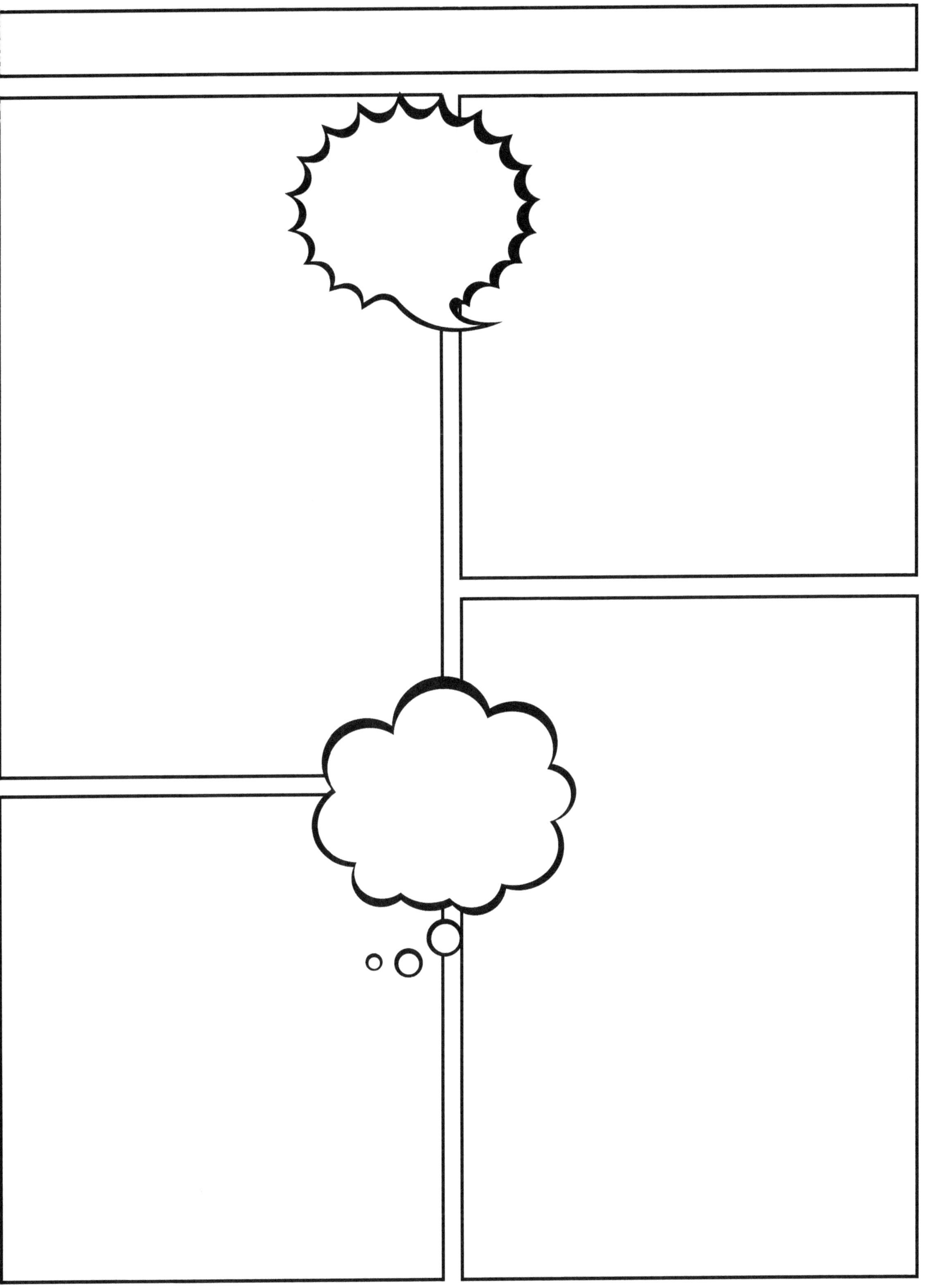

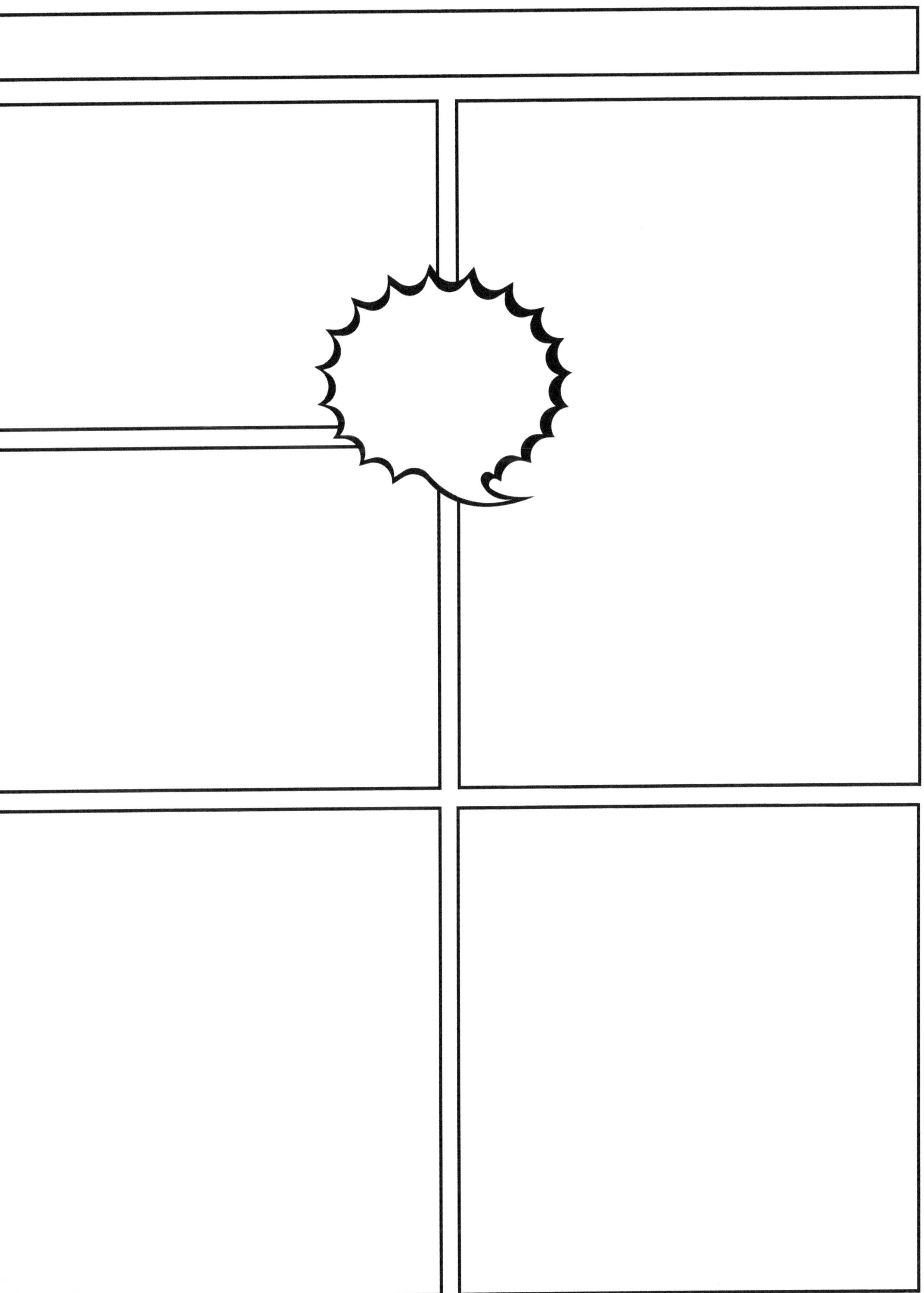

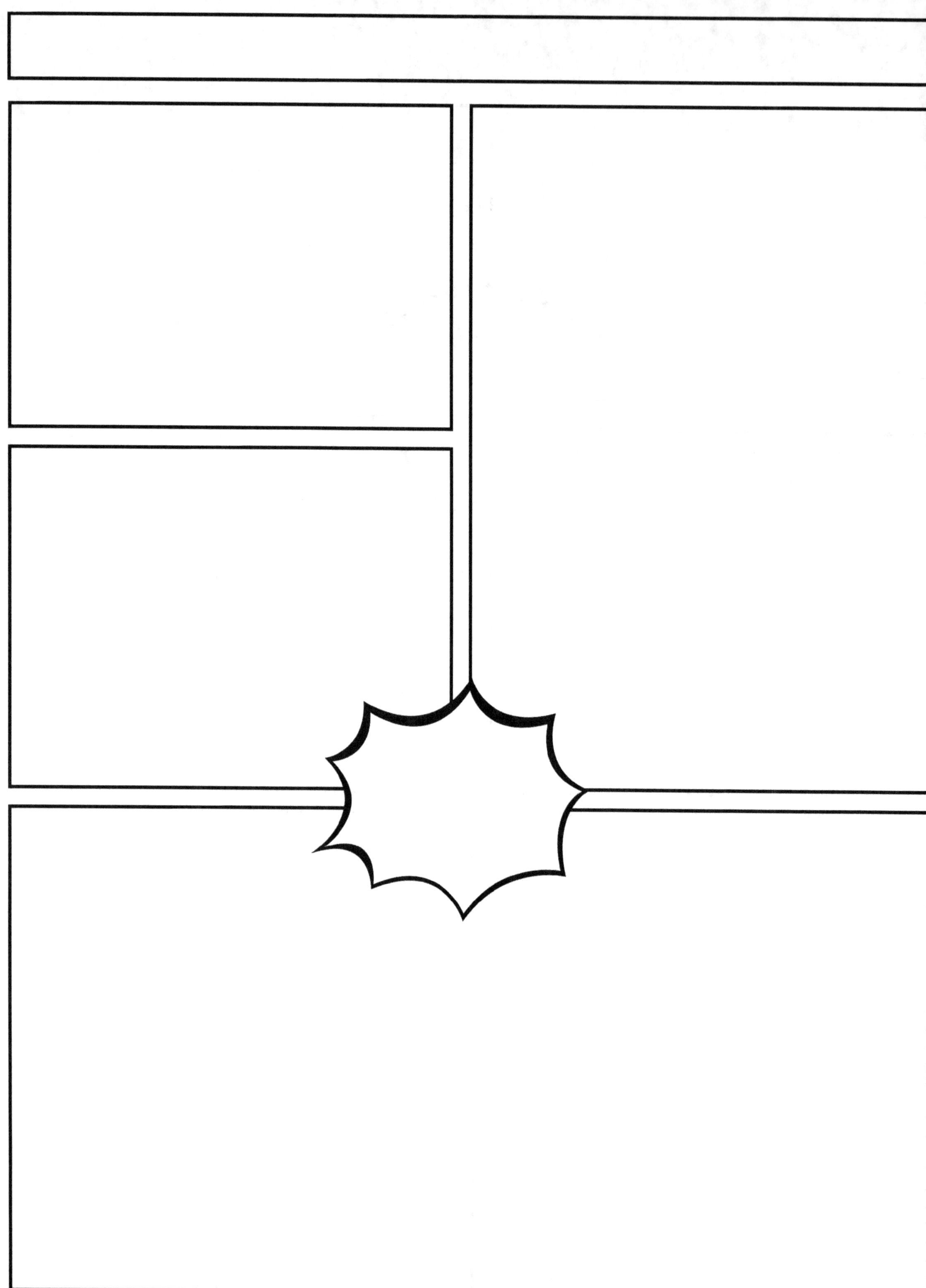

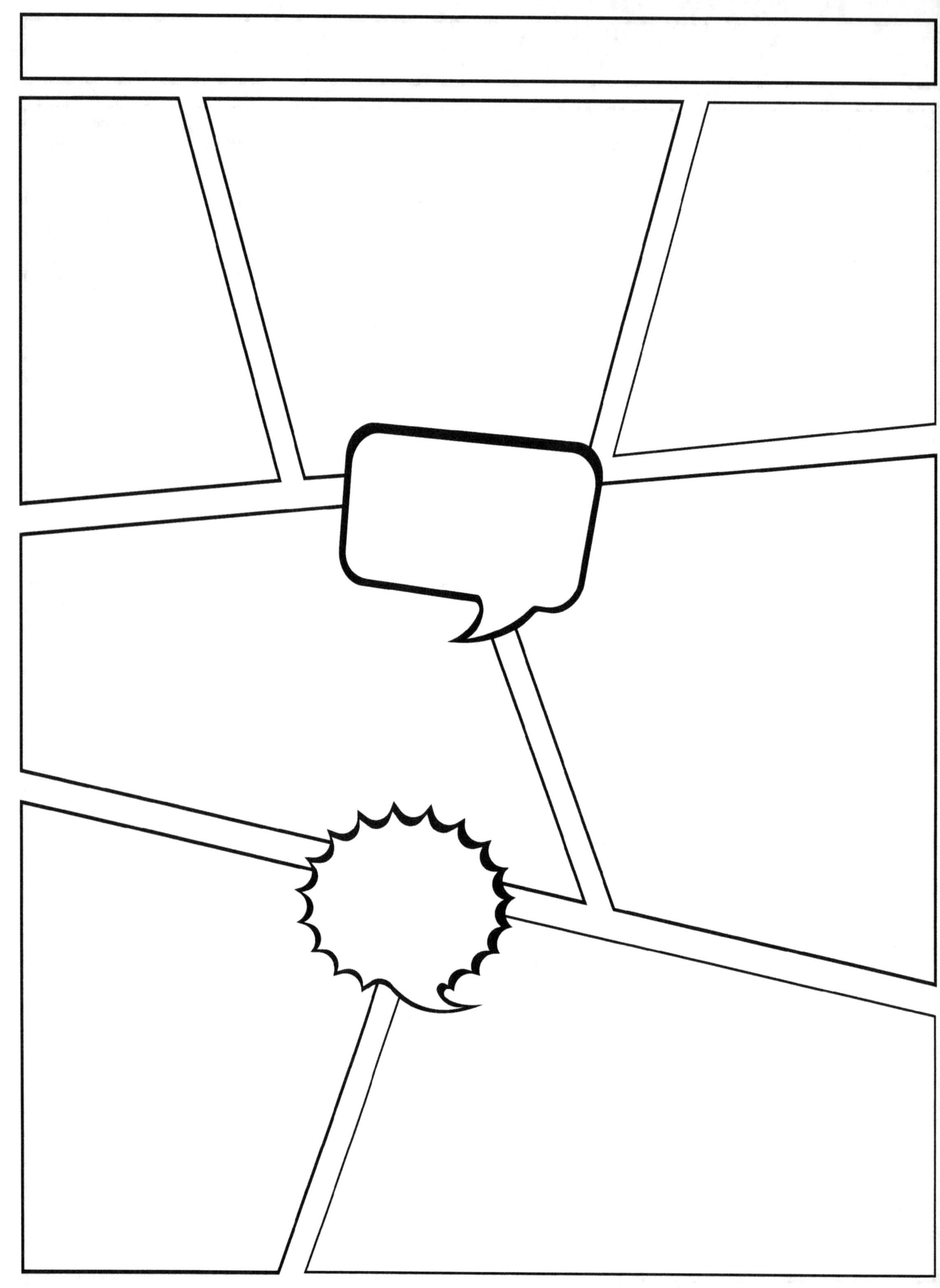

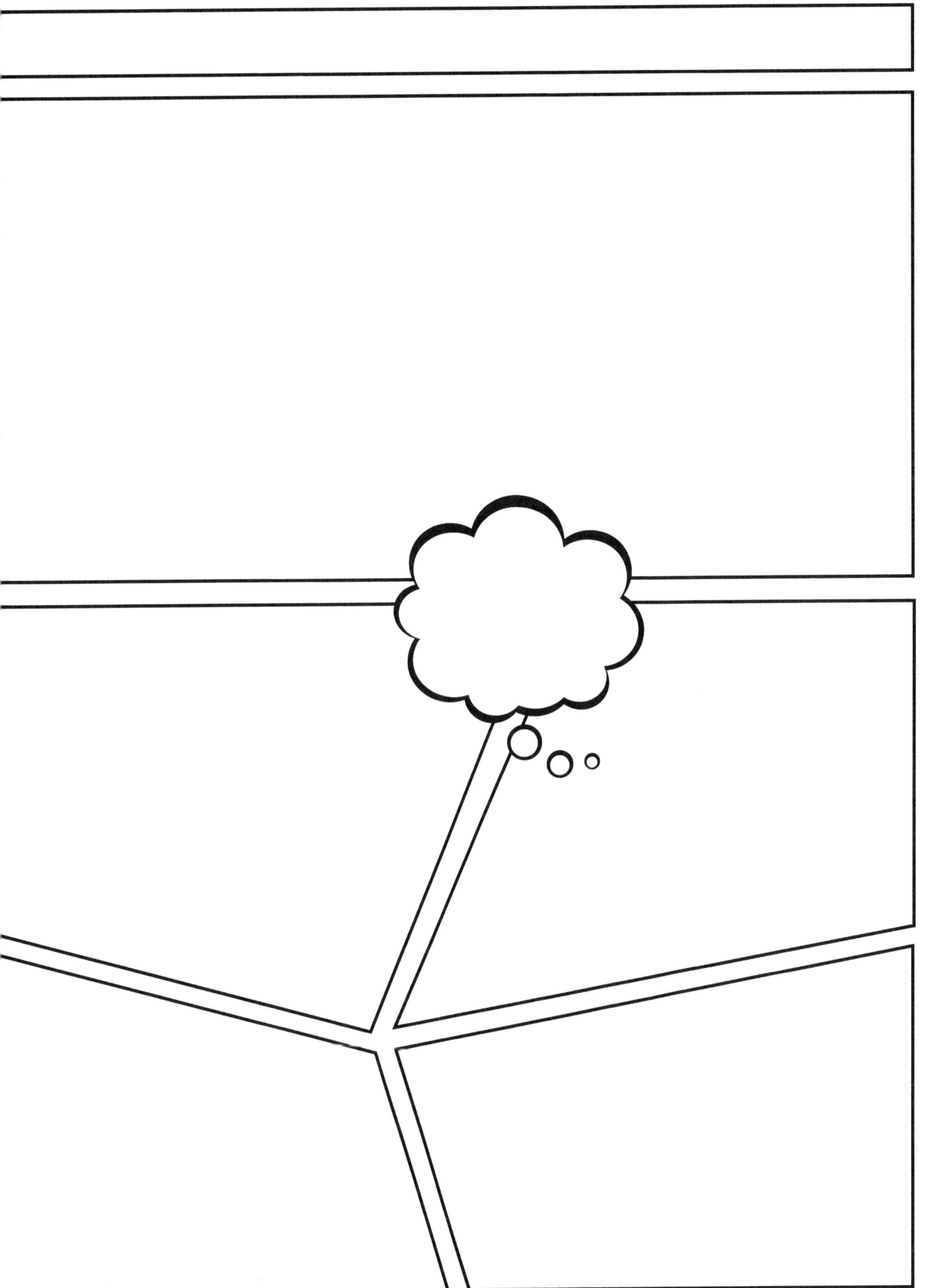

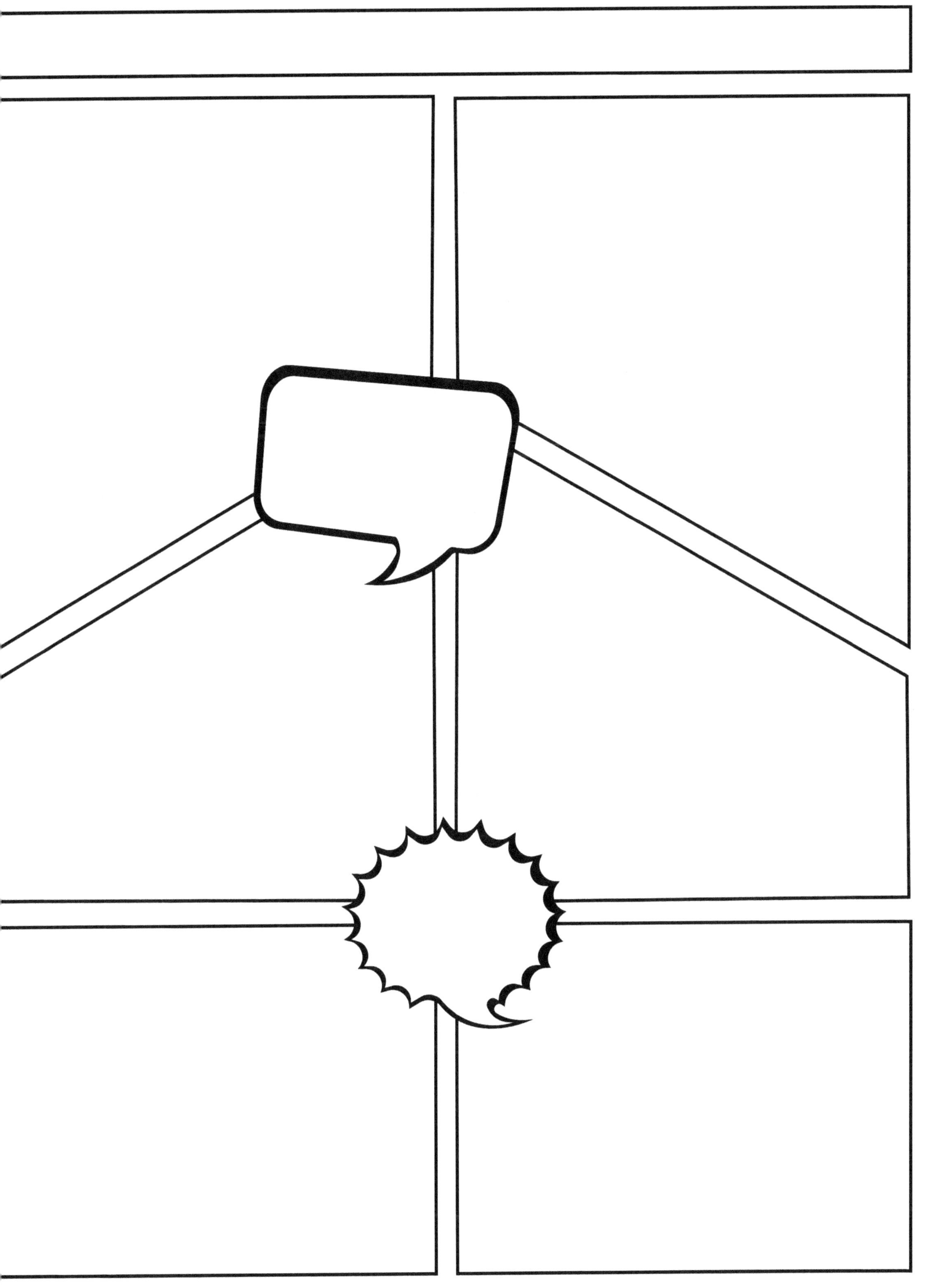

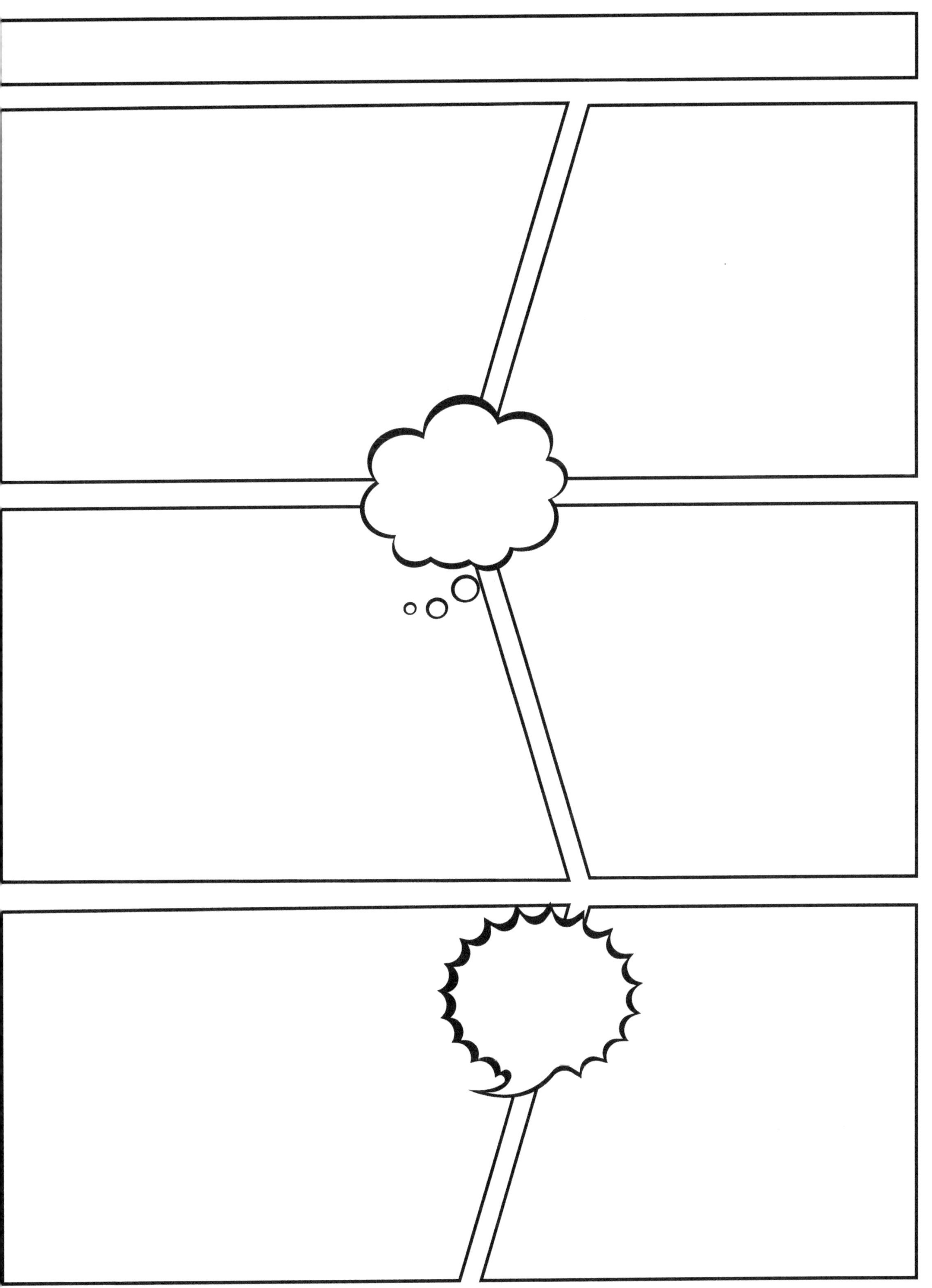

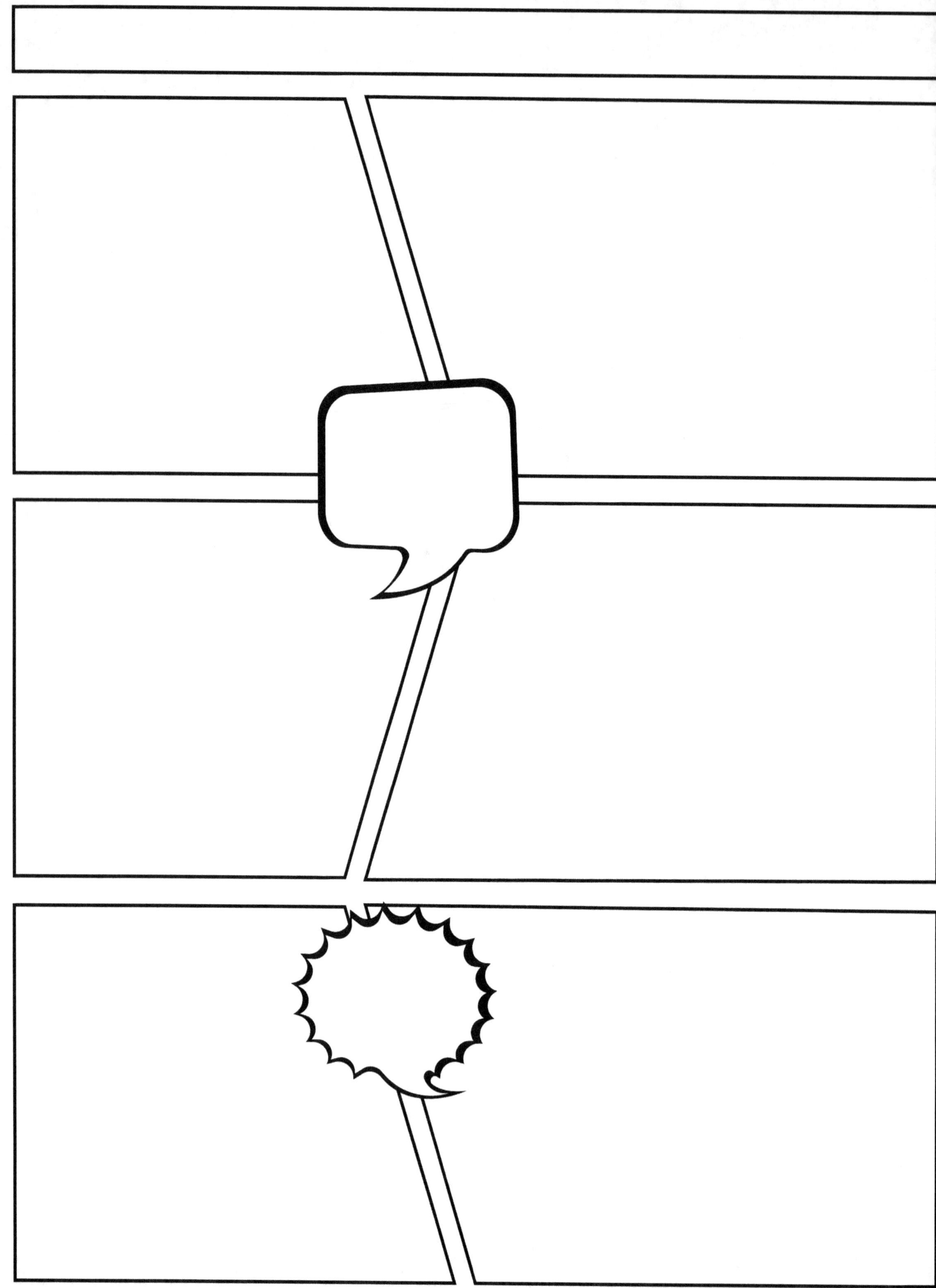

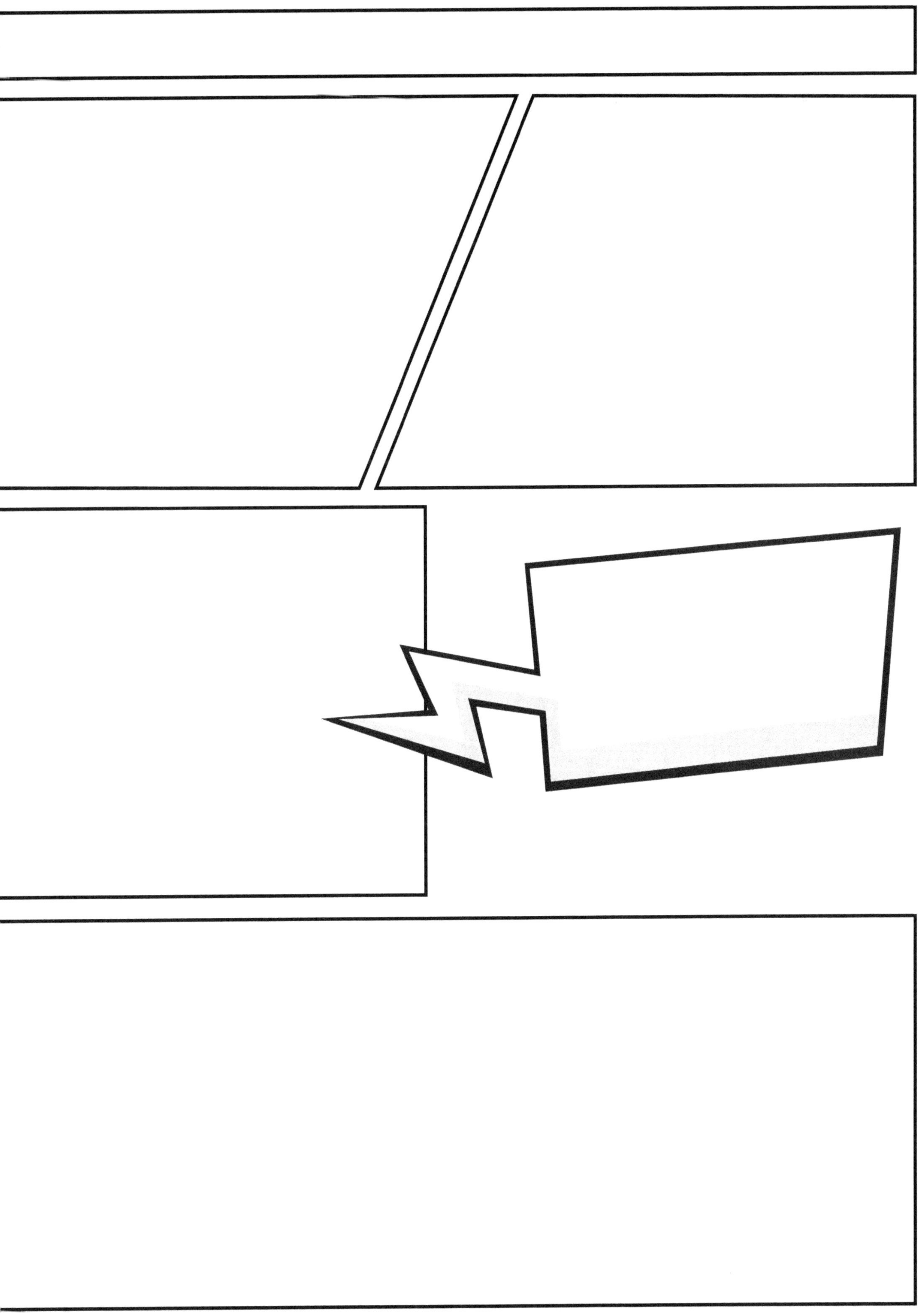

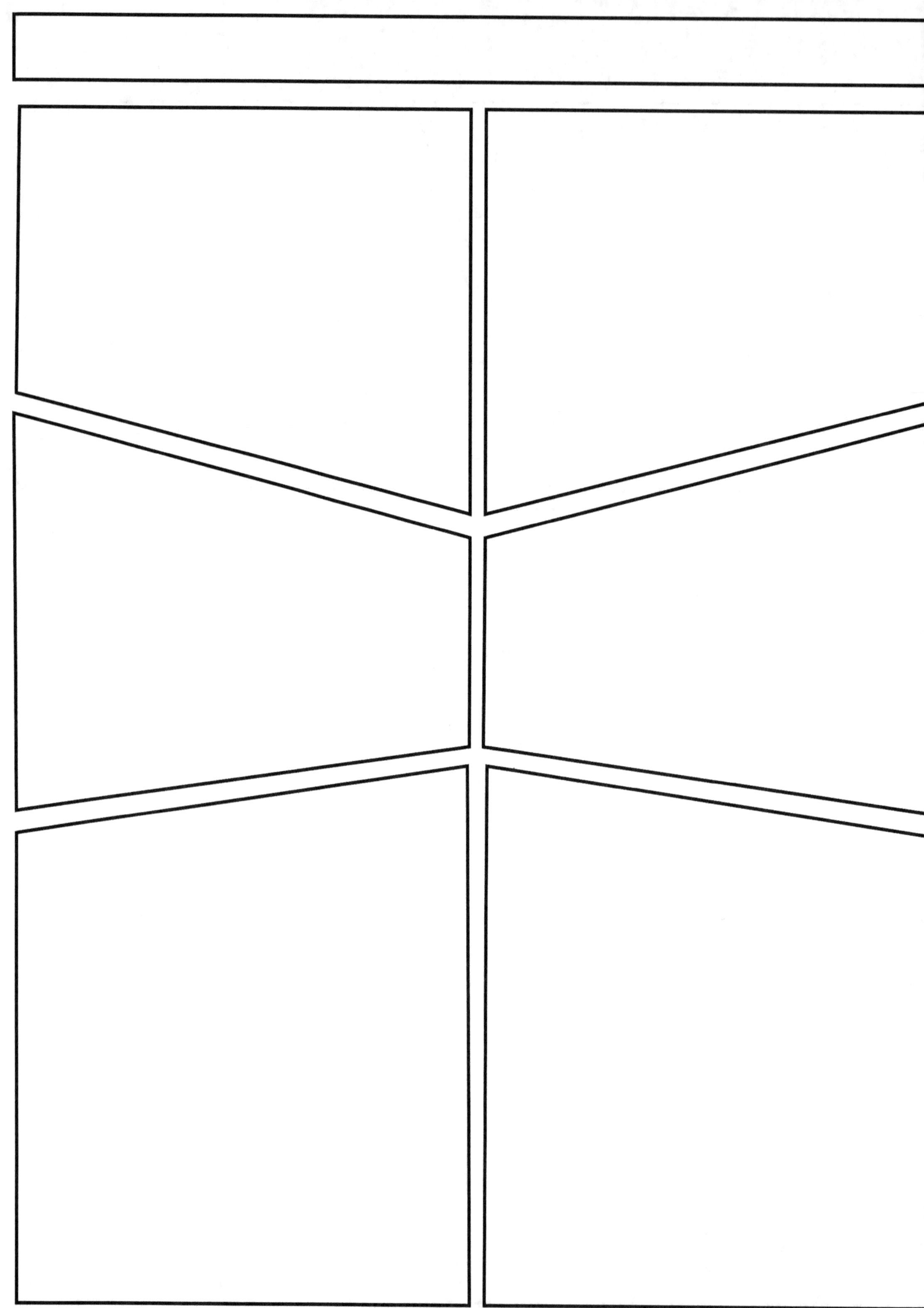

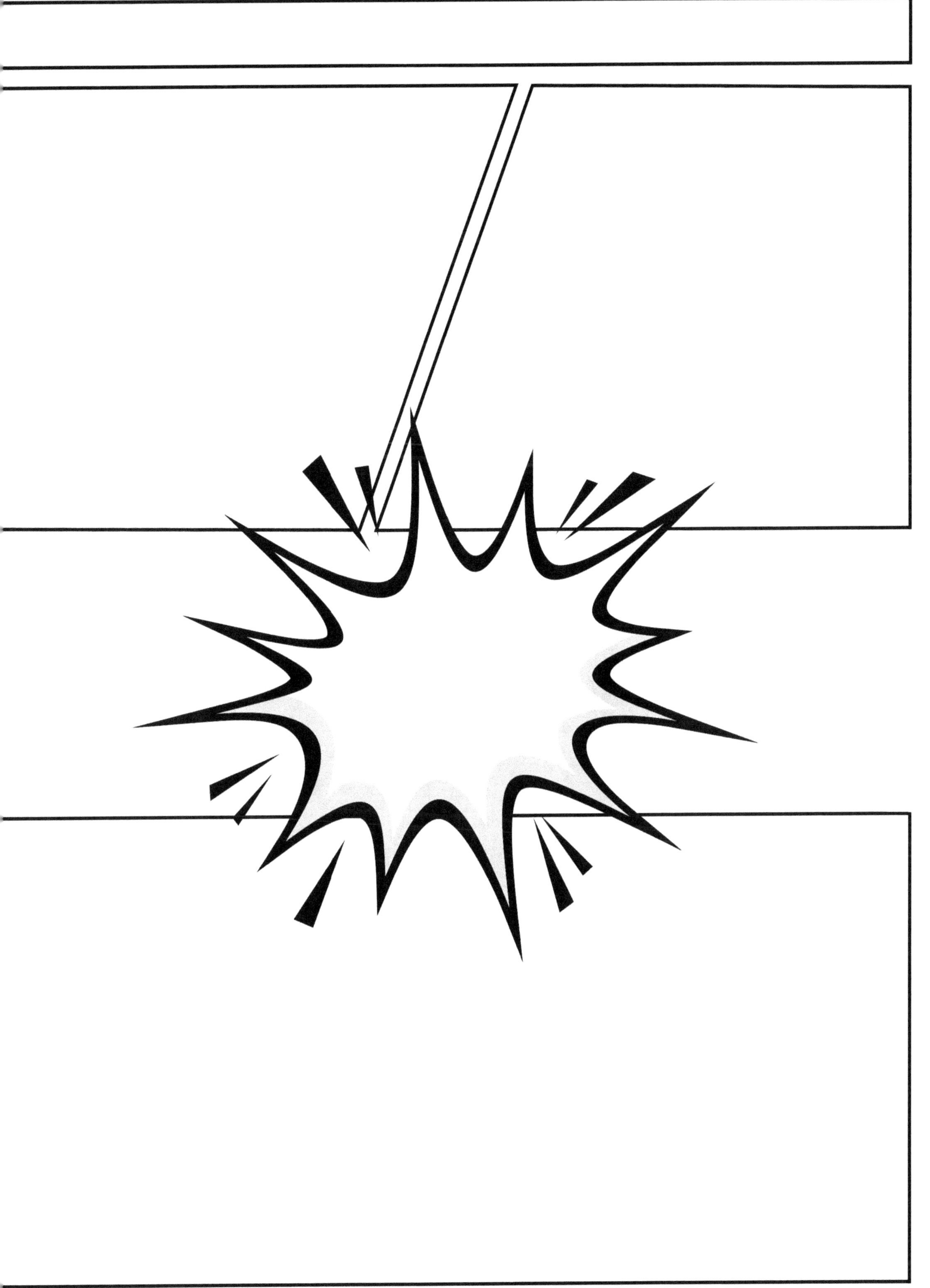

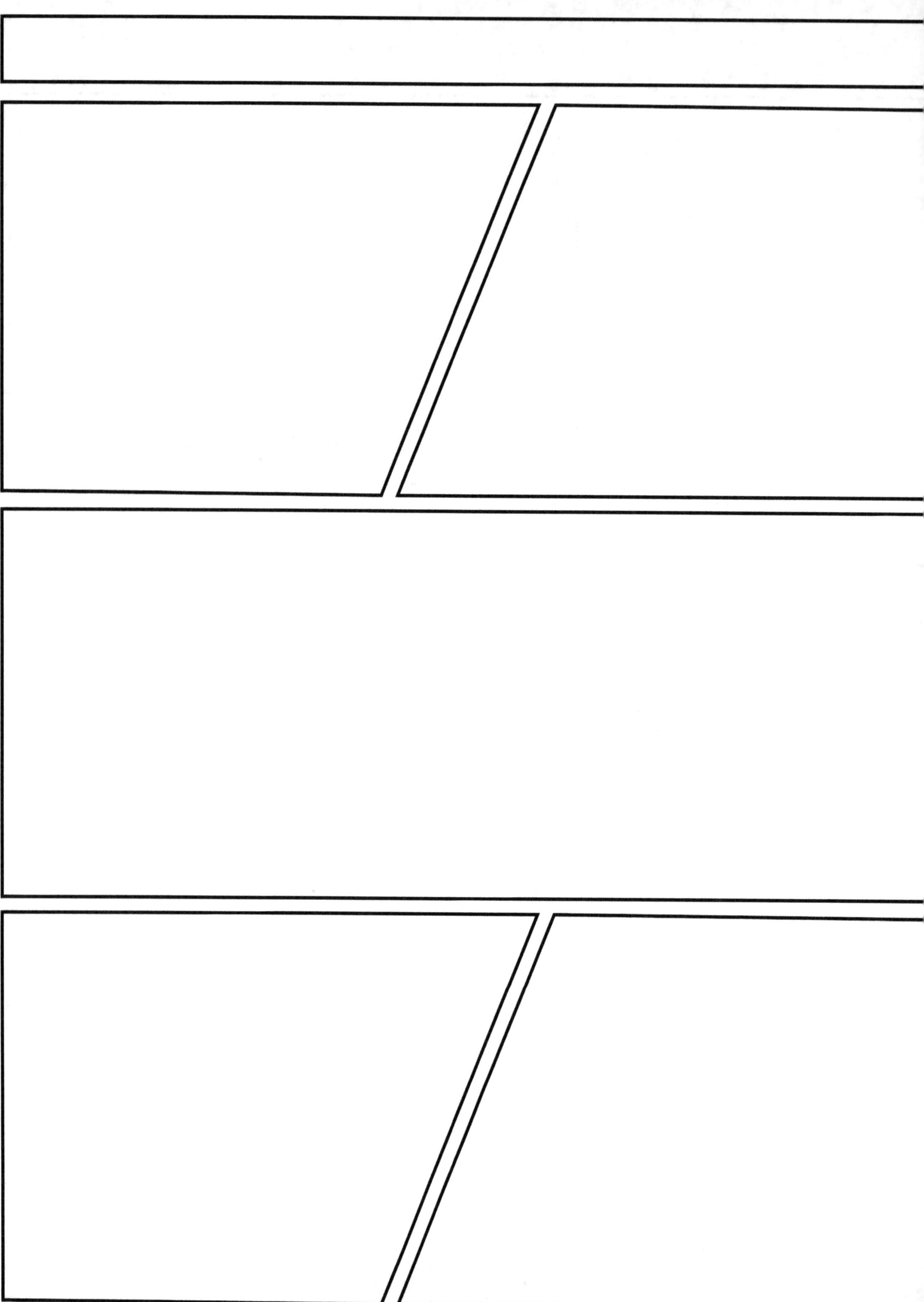

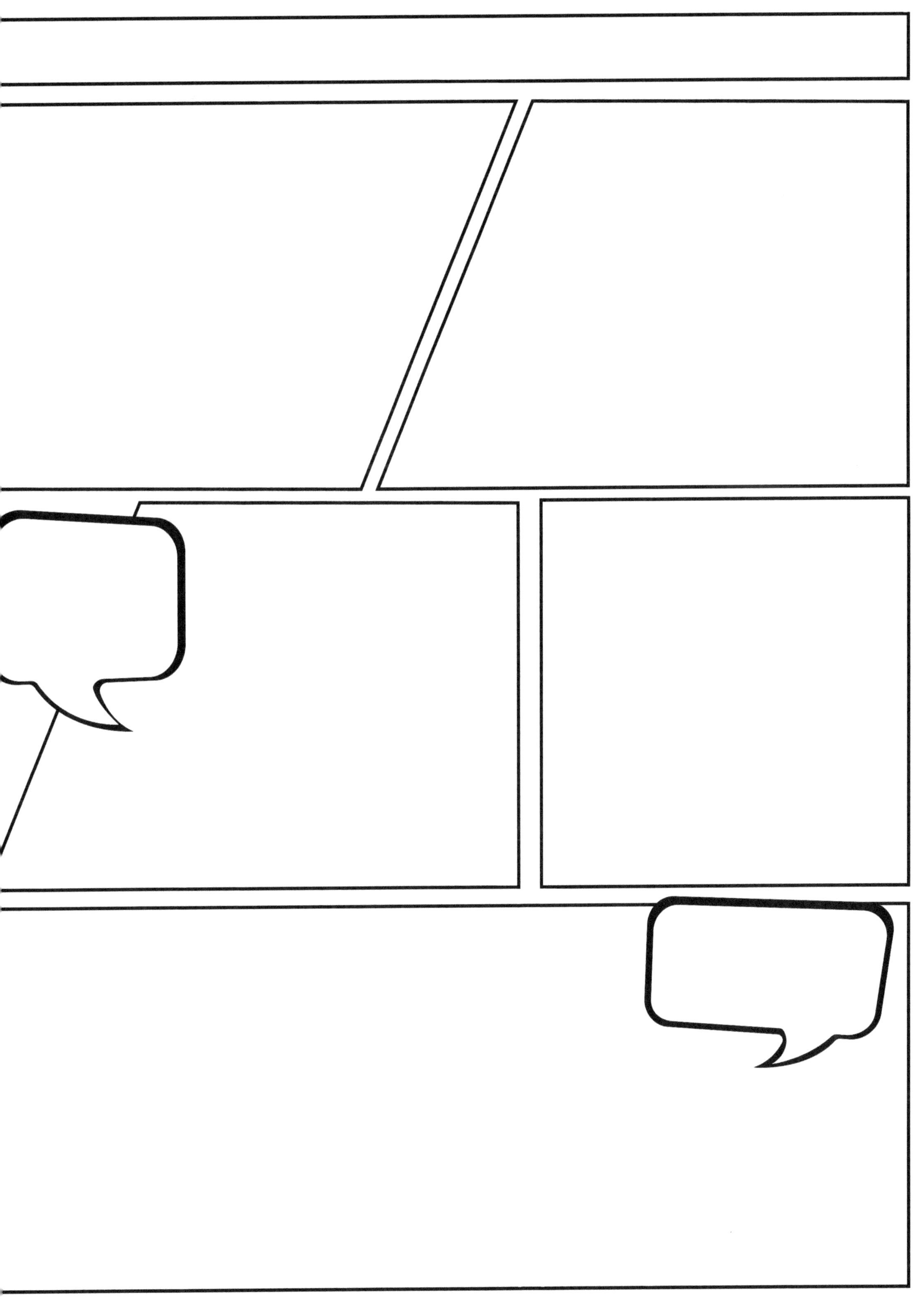

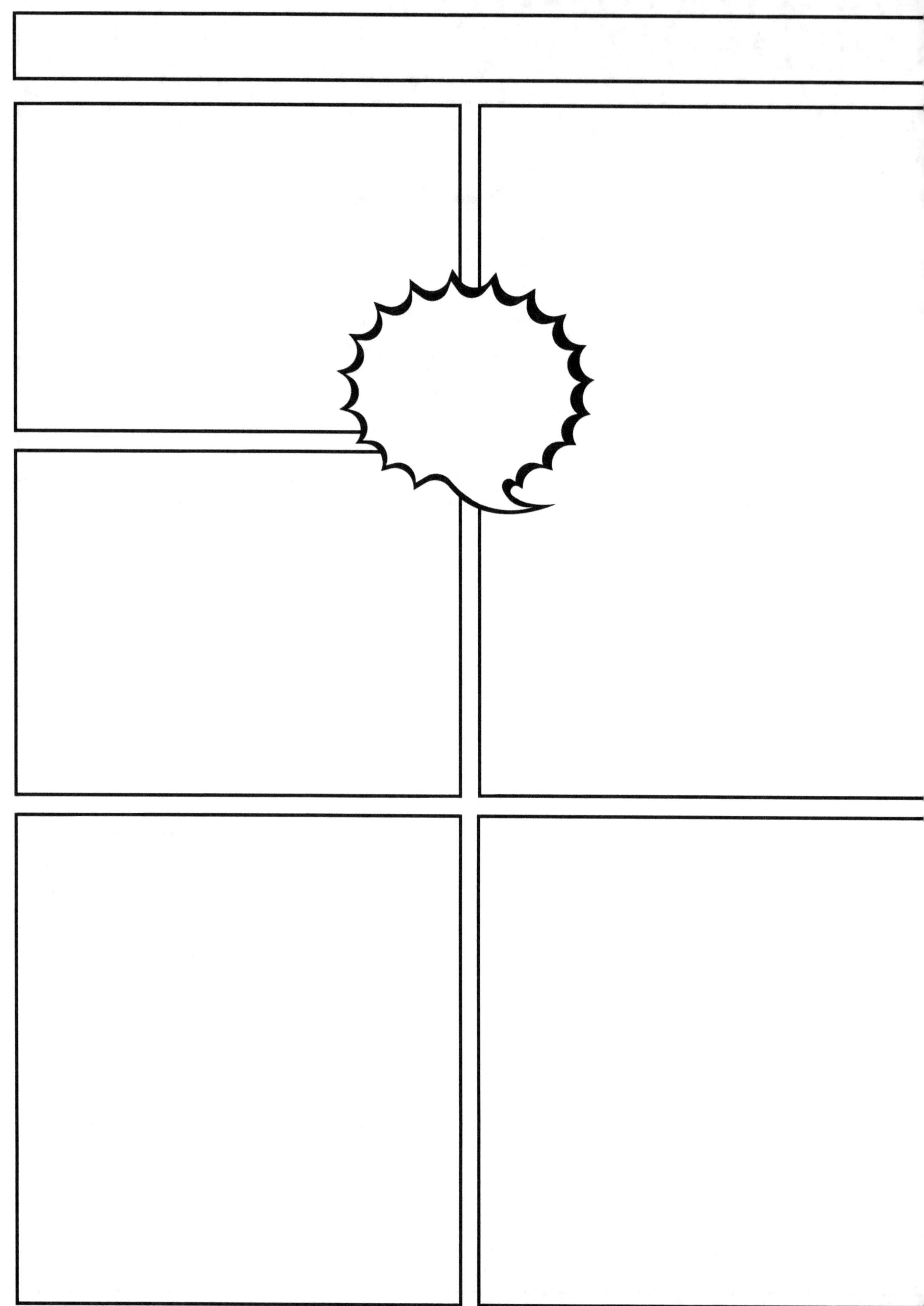

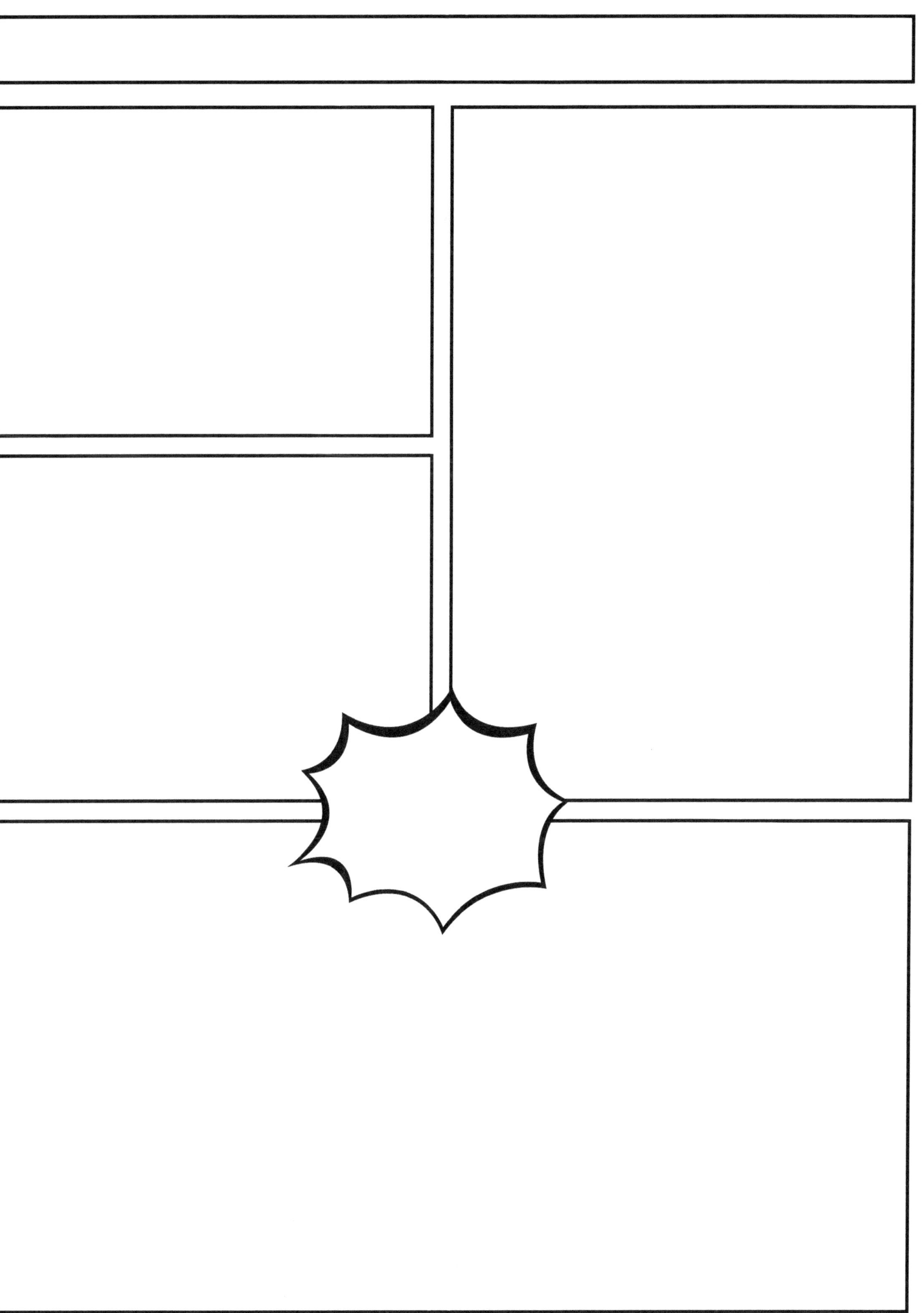

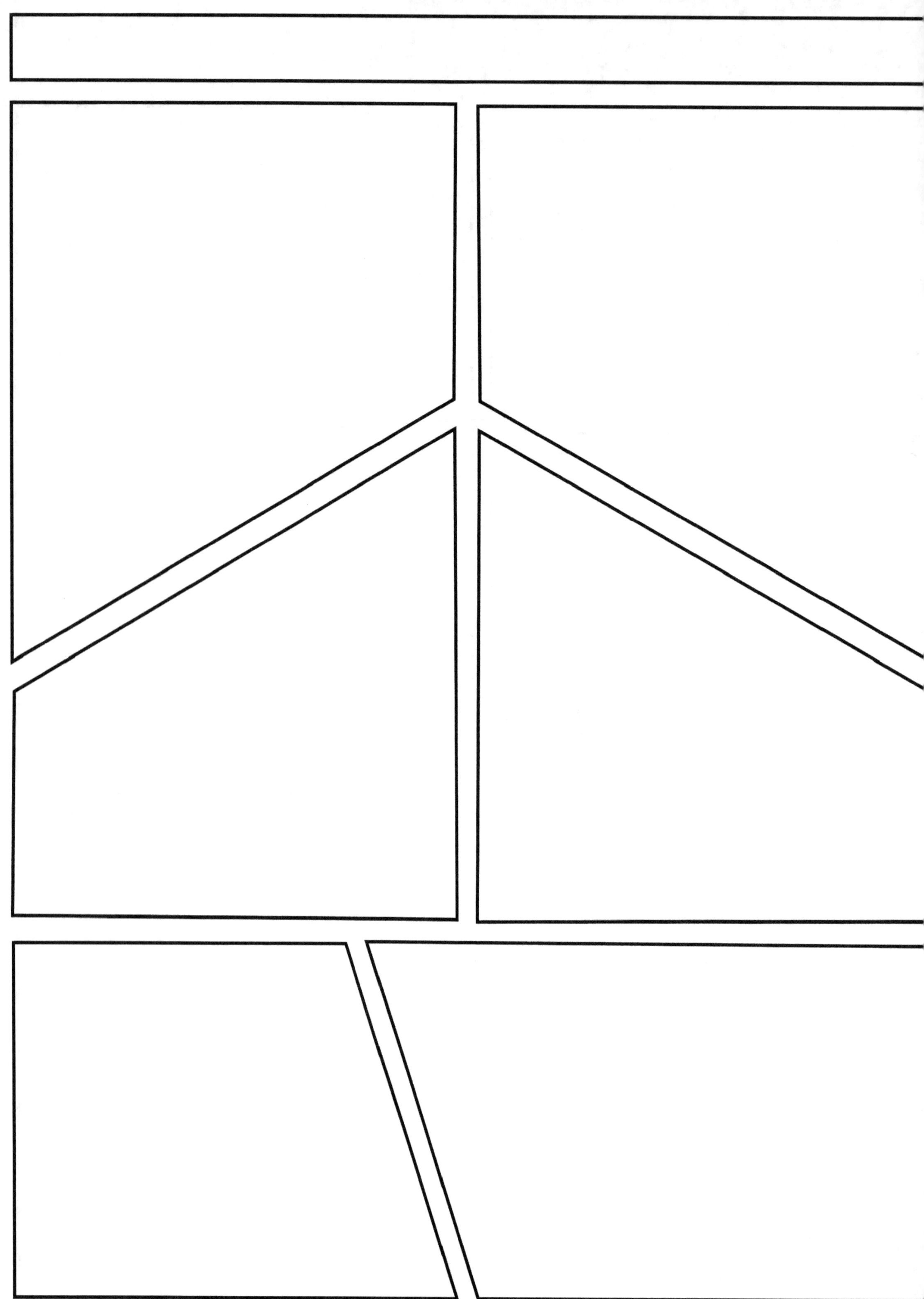

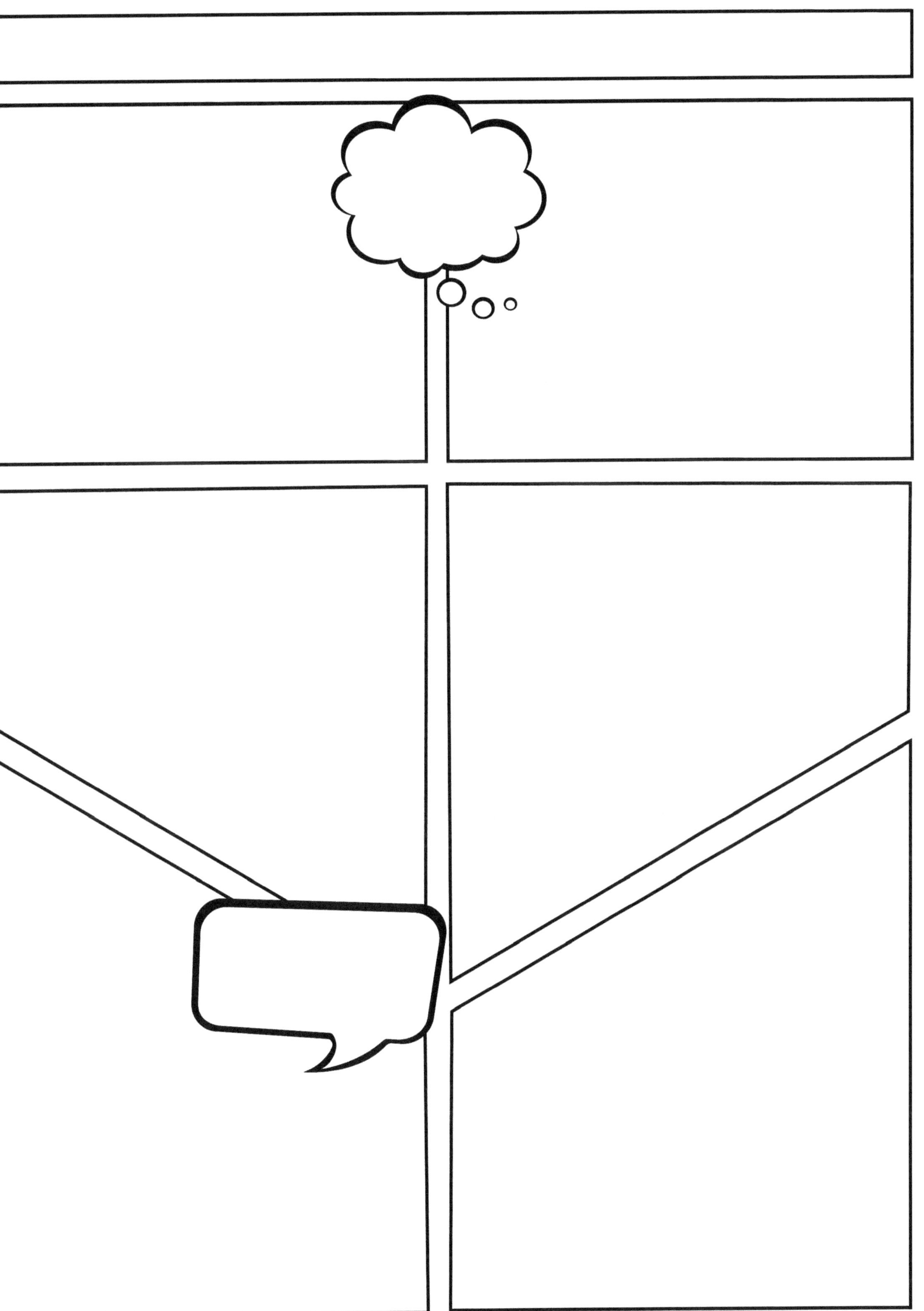

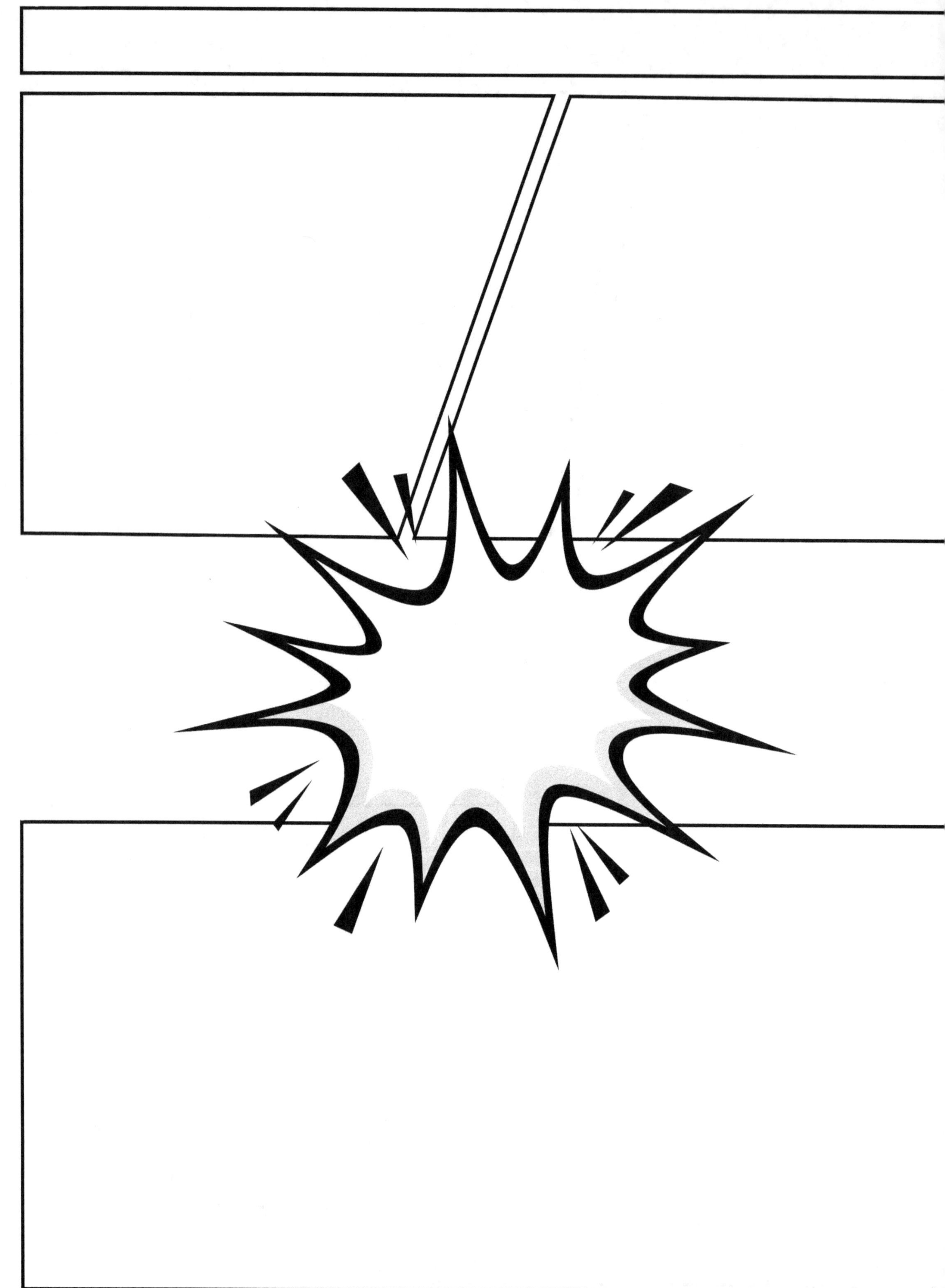

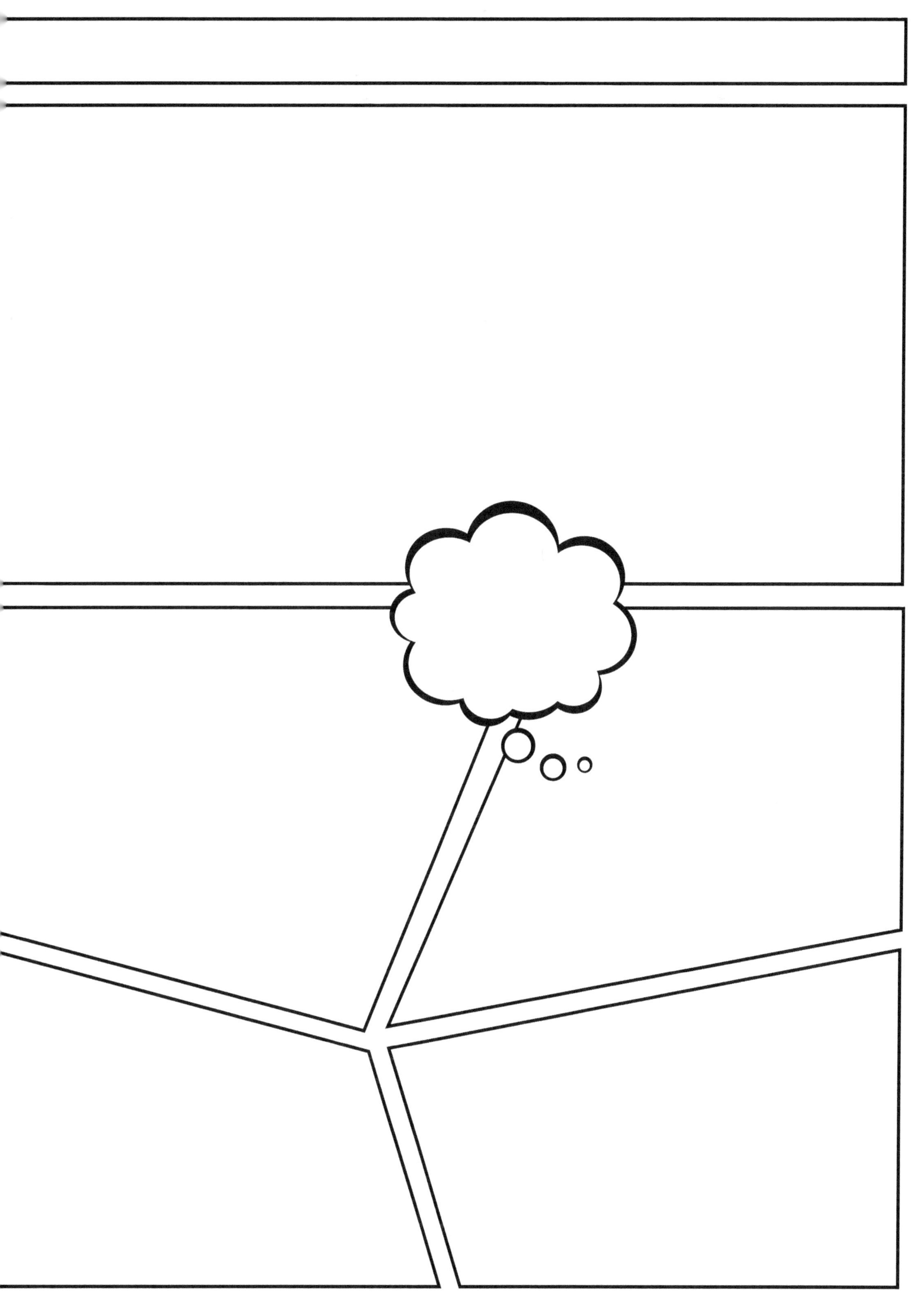

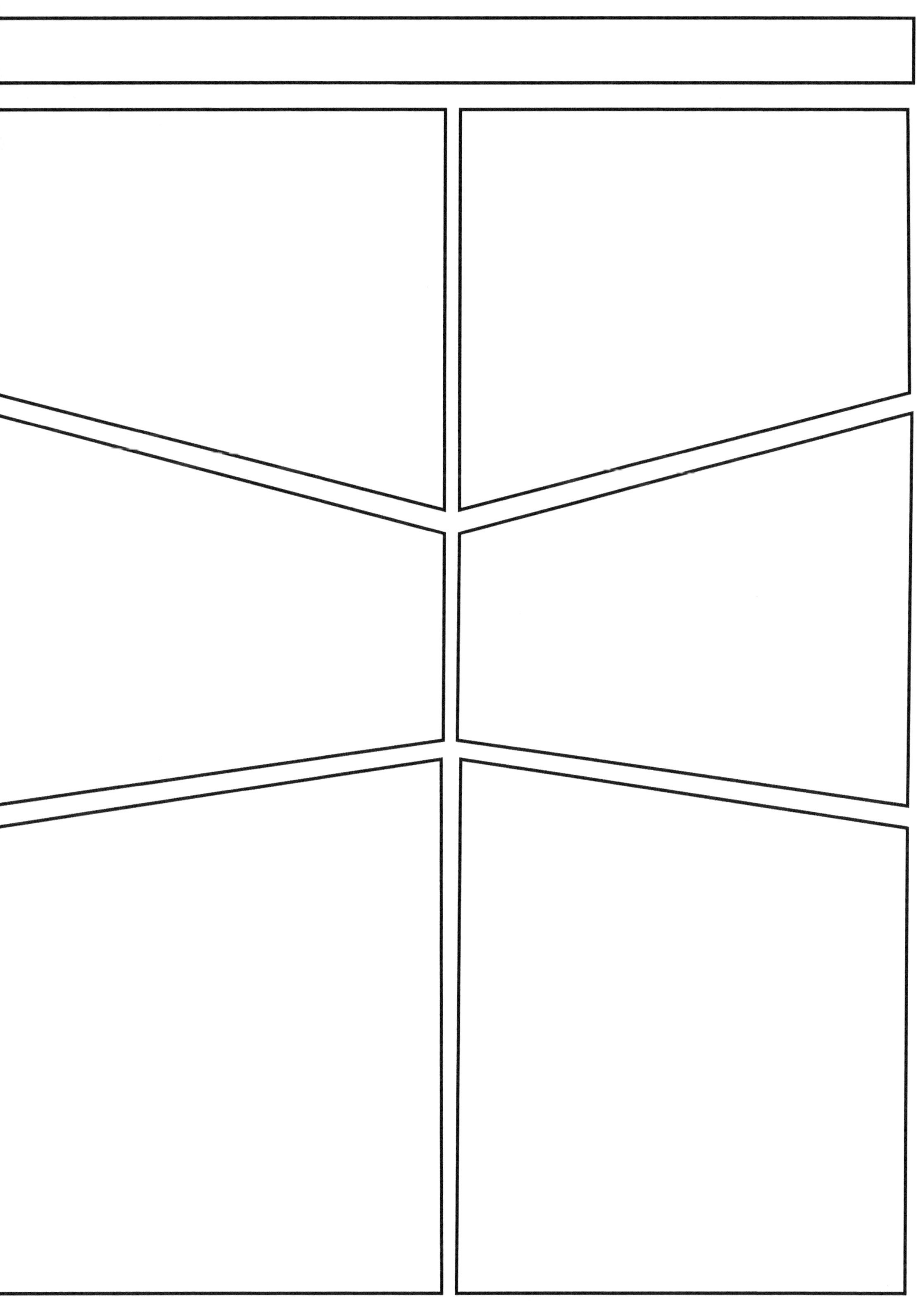

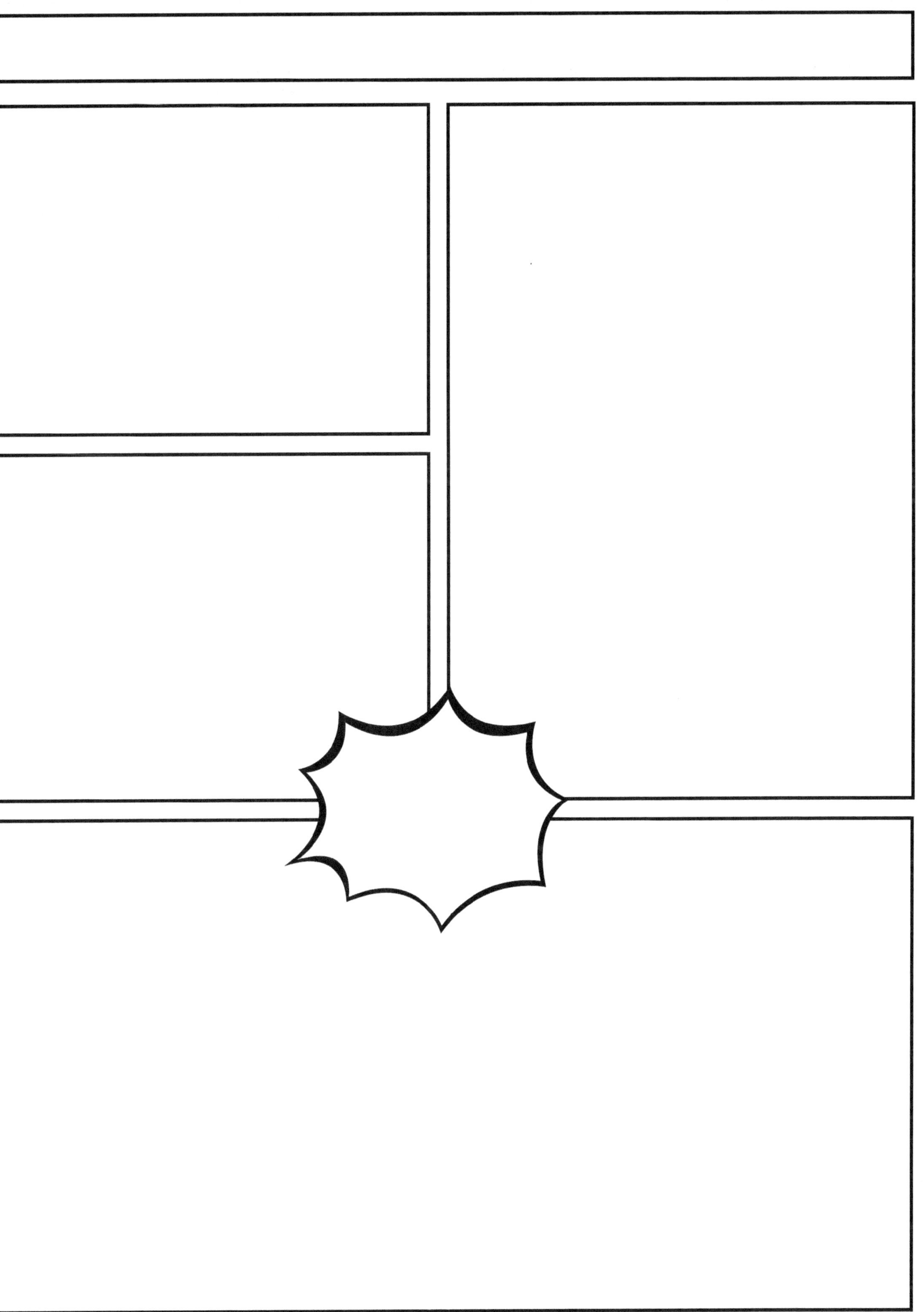

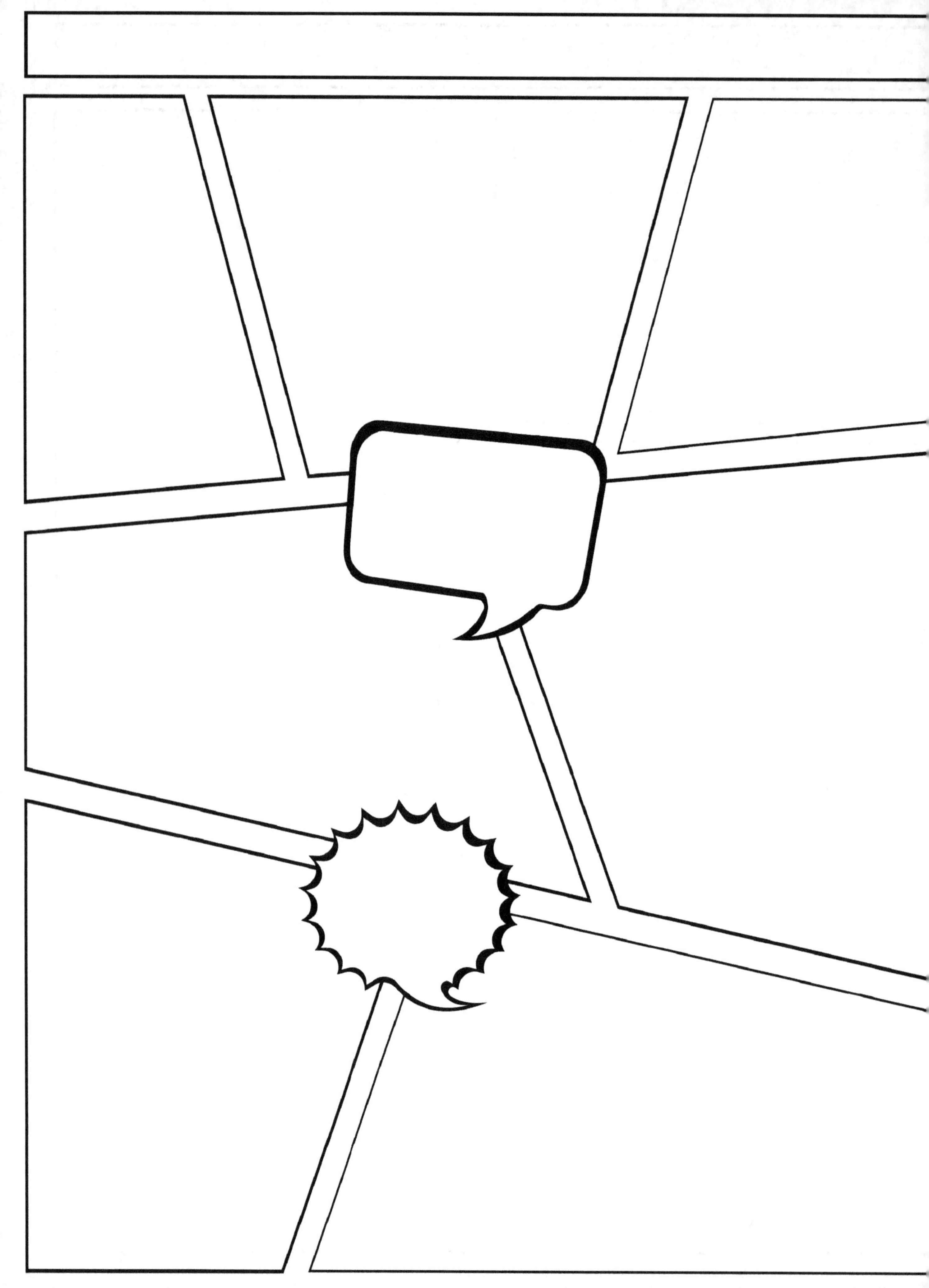

Bonus
Notebook
Comics

We hope you enjoyed our book

As a small family company, your feedback is very important to us.

Please let us know how you like our book at :

promobileamz@gmail.com

KIDS PLAY COMICS